Human Manipulation:
An Introduction to Social Psychology

Human Manipulation:
An Introduction to Social Psychology

Chris Park

JPark Publishing
2015

JPark Self Publishing © 2015 by Chris Park

All rights reserved. This book or any portion thereof may not be reproduced or used in any manner whatsoever without the express written permission of the publisher except for the use of brief quotations in a book review or scholarly journal.

First Printing: 2015

ISBN 978-1-329-15293-9
Chris' Self Publication
Email: junoo.park@gmail.com

Dedication

Thank you to Ms. Elie, without you I wouldn't have ever thought of completing a non-fiction book of my own.
Thank you to Mr. Tjosvold, for helping me through the final publishing stage.

Contents

Preface..xi
Conformity 3
Diversion of Responsibility 13
Obedience to Authority 22
Other Uses and Experiments about Obedience to Authority 34
Deception of Mind 40
The Deceiving in Our Beliefs 54
Psychological Selfishness 66
Reciprocity 70
Deceiving in the Marketing Industry 74
References 83

Preface

Humans have existed for more than 200,000 years, and we were intelligent but physically disadvantaged animals. With only our intelligence, we could not do much, since without resources, nothing practical could be done. Therefore we had to be in groups to survive in the harsh worlds, to defend ourselves and survive as a species, and this book will describe our evolutionary changes in the social life that still affects us now in the modern society.

This book just gives a short glimpse of our social-psychological selves, providing interesting ideas, concepts, and experiments. It does not include complicated details about the major in science, and is aimed for the people who know little or nothing about psychology, giving them opinions about the topic. However, if one is looking for a deep through book about psychology, then one may close this book, since: firstly, it is a very short book compared to other scientific books, secondly, it does not provide deep, through information about the topic, and finally, if one has already studied this topic, they will find much known information in this particular book.

If this is not you, this book will grasp you in the scarcely known subject, since many events dealing with this subject may come as intriguing, psychopathic, funny, or even terrifying.

Chris Park

Conformity

Humans were very weak animals compared to other animals in most parts of our history, and in individuals we could not survive. Therefore, groups were made to protect each other, each with a specialty. As an example, one might gather food, while one hunts, and others defend their territory from other animals. Each of them did not want to get others unpleased, since the group would fall apart and they would be left alone. So to please others, we have developed our ability to obey, otherwise said conform to others.

This might feel very untrue for some of the readers, since when words like obey, or conform is heard, we do not like it. In western cultures, we like to be unique and extraordinary. Therefore these might give one negative thoughts like mass producing equalized robots, but it is better to think of as a group of friends agreeing on an interesting debate. This, yet will still be not enough to change someone's opinion, and research has shown that we think ourselves as unique and different individuals with powerful self-opinions than we actually are.

There are many experiments to show this, one of the most famous being the Asch's experiment. The experiment took place in 1951, making it one of the earliest social psychology experiments. The experiment is as following. There were people asked to answer a simple set of questions like this.

A Short Introduction to Social Psychology

They were told that it was a visual testing experiment. However, anyone with normal eyesight could see the answer, it is

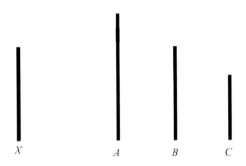

Which line is equivalent to line X? Line A, B, or C?

extremely obvious; it is line B. However, only one third of the people tested had answered it correctly, and they were average people, not unintelligent, physical, or mentally challenged. They were just impacted by the situational power.

The situation was made so there were six people answering the questions, but only one was the true 'participant' of the experiment, and the rest were actors ordered to say the wrong answer. By the actors saying the wrong answer, it had given the participant pressure. However, more than just saying the wrong answer was done, but the actors would give speechless peer pressure, by staring at them, getting him/her into center of attention. If one were to tell the correct answer, he/she would be discomforted would feel to be the outsider of the 'wrong answer community'. If as the reader, you are going *'I wouldn't do that. That is a very incomprehensible act'* after reading this, then that would be haughtiness, since in these kinds of situational power, it has been proven that you won't know what you will do when put in to the situation. If you are thinking that the changed social norms and environment how people think since 1951, that's a wrong hypothesis, since this famous experiment had been repeated multiple times and the result only had a slight change, with little tolerance.

A Short Introduction to Social Psychology

This experiment may seem like nothing except that people might err in questions knowing the answers, but it has way more to do with conformity. Conformity is a huge part in social psychology, since it is dealt with how we obey others even though we tend to think ourselves as very individualistic. However, conformity does not end here, and farther into this there are many deaths involved too. As an example, in South Korea there was a fire in a subway train. Much smoke and carbon monoxide was released, but the surprising factor is that there was a very low number of people that had evacuated. When psychologists researched this odd happening, the answer to the phenomenon was conformity. Since other people were acting fine inside a smoking subway train, no one had the urge to get out, and be the odd one.

The brain releases calming hormones when others are calm in an alarming situation, and this was the negative uses of that. Those other people were feeling fine because they had a person in authority, the subway driver. He was calm, and he broadcasted that the train was safe, and the train will get going in a matter of minutes. However, the driver, after looking at all the smoke had ran away from the subway, leaving the people to die without hope.

Experimenters, after knowing about the incident, decided to conduct an experiment where they had six people in a room, and told them they had an average survey and had given ten minutes to answer it. The independent variable is that in about a few minutes, they had let smoke fill up the room with a fake smoke maker. It was to check if anyone got out. They had put the people in one place, and five of the six were actors told to act calm and only one person was actually being tested at a time. It was a basic replica of the shocking subway incident. The time was made to be ten minutes, since it was the time it took for carbon monoxide in real smoke to harm the body. The result (predictable, since it is also equivalent to Asch's Experiment) was that nobody who were being tested got out even when the room was completely filled with smoke and no one was able to see a foot ahead. To see if this experiment was due to social effects, they repeated the experiment where the person was alone, and the result assured that it was due to social effects; hence the people had left the room in average of eleven seconds.

Asch's experiment is very valuable in the social psychology world as it explains many absurd things people may do and what our culture might see disturbing or odd, but is the nature of the human kind.

There was another experiment conducted about conformity and how people act if put in certain situations. It was led by psychology Professor Zimbardo at Stanford University, and the experiment called the Stanford Prison Experiment. As the name may tell, the professor had made a fake prison somewhere in Stanford

University. They needed people to be in the prison, and they scouted some people to be prison guards and some people to be the criminals to be in the prison and they had done this by draw, 12 men for each roles to be exact. The people who were involved in this experiment, like many experiments, completely average if not more intelligent people had been scouted. It was to test if it was the stereotypical personality traits of the guards and the criminals that made the abusive behavior happen.

The experiment had to be stopped abruptly in 6 days, which is less than half the duration supposed. The hypothesis was more than accurate, and a rather terrifying result was seen. People who were involved, 12 men who were guards, was physically and mentally abusing the men they did not know a week ago, as if it was in real prison. Some of the prisoners were passively accepting that it was okay to be abused since they were prisoners. The guards were ordering to abuse and strip the people who neglected. It was quite a shocking experiment, but again, they were not psychopaths; but average humans like us, and it was proof that we get overpowered by situation.

Many people after seeing this happen, would have thought that 'I wouldn't do such a thing', since we tend to think ourselves higher than other people and morally more accurate. Easily said, we love ourselves. Therefore, after looking at the horrific results, after 30 years the experiment was done, without intention, a similar situation had happened, and the results were very similar. It was in Abu Ghraib Prison, where the people, normal soldiers and the prisoners of war, were giving and getting the exact same treatment as the Stanford Prison Experiment. The prisoners were getting stripped, guards and fellow prisoners were hitting, jumping on other prisoners. It was complete abuse, and those people themselves didn't think that they would be doing such inhumane things.

It is natural to see the most shocking part would be people turning so violent other people, but on the other hand, it can be also very surprising that others were accepting the fact that it was permissible for the prison guards or the American soldiers to take such actions. There were many who stood up for themselves, but that only resulted in more forceful harm. Therefore giving that permission to harm was a very dangerous decision, and a very negative one, but why had the prisoners let the guards harm them?

Another research has shown that one feels much pain when non-conforming, which is similar to physical pain, and the brain sends out negative hormones. Conforming is one of our brain's way of making us feel good. The reason for this might be that since the olden days, we could not live alone without getting killed, or nowadays unemployed without getting along and getting other people's help. Therefore, teamwork and group management are playing an important role in human society, and conformity is the one of the many ways our brain adopted to accommodate to this.

Chris Park

Diversion of Responsibility

In our society, we live with such a big number of other people that we don't even know all the people in our community. We have developed quite an odd way to accommodate this, which might seem psychopathic, but research says you will act the same too. As the title says, the way is diversion of responsibility, and it is where the responsibility to help others or do things is diverted and everyone expects that others will do it.

As an example, a student in a school may drop their items; quite too much to handle by themselves, and other's help would be very supportive. People think most people are kind enough to help, and everyone think they will if put in the correct situation. Therefore depending on what situation someone is put, their reaction may differ quite a lot.

A Short Introduction to Social Psychology

When researched, results were saying was that people, if alone were very likely to help than if they were in a group of people. It was that if they were in groups, people thought to each other that someone was going to do it even though it can be clearly seen that none of them were, since they were also thinking equally. In fact if there were six or more people in a group the possibility of helping was none. However, the possibility of someone helping alone was 85 percent. That is a very high rate, considering that the reason they hadn't helped was probably because they were late for a meeting or something somewhat important.

This result, like many other social psychology results might seem very unimportant, but situations have happened where people have died in a hospital due to a heart attack because no one had helped, even with nurses and doctors passing by. What was the reason? There were many witnesses, and all the witness had experienced Diversion of Responsibility at the time. As you may have recognized, it also is a phenomenon when one thinks they do not have the responsibility or others have already taken responsibility, not just people not helping others. The condition occurs when there are many people in a group, and it is shown to be effective with three or more people in a group. As the writer I believe the phenomenon occurs because even though helping others are a good deed, there might be negative results if they help, and no direct positive results occur while helping. The phenomenon also be the reason why turn in rates are so low for small crimes like drink-and-driving.

However, this does not mean that nobody will be there to help you when you are in danger, since when explicitly told to help, then almost everyone will offer to help. This does not mean everyone will help in a dangerous event where much negative results might occur by helping but rather helping someone picking up their utensils. The level of explicitly needed might be just calling their names, to giving step by step directions what to do. What makes the difference is the level of risk it takes to help. The risk, if one is about to argue there might be none, there are always many unexpected events. For example, in China, by helping a wounded get to a hospital, the helper was accused of the harm and was sent to jail. This example is set to extreme and most likely not to happen to most people, however, it shows there are certain levels of social risk in every action taken.

With all this information, one might wonder, what starts this phenomenon? The simple answer would be that when one starts to feel that they are in a group, and associated with them by some direct or indirect way, one will think any responsibility is not there, or theirs. Specifically, when one is with 3 or more people, one starts to feel that they are in a group and associated with them. It does not simply stop there, the range of how responsible they are differs between the numbers of people they are with. The more people there are in a group the less responsible one feels, and less serious the help or the problem the less responsible they feel. Again, the more serious the problem means more risk and a better chance off without taking it. Therefore in a public place, where there are many people, the responsibility is diverted very much with others. For example, not much people will actually turn in people harassing others in subways and busses, because there is an unconscious thought in the back of people's head 'someone is going to do it'. The more responsible they will feel with less people like in a room with no one but 2 people, it is sure someone is going to help a person having a heart attack. But again, in a hospital a person had died because of this phenomenon.

A Short Introduction to Social Psychology

However, people who defy this phenomenon has been seen, and these people were considered 'heroes' that we can see in newspapers and articles. The people who sacrificed themselves for others were considered very big heroes, these people would get awarded honors acknowledging their help and the honor unto them. The meaning of sacrifice in this paragraph doesn't need to be dying in a war, since it does not go along with the concept of this phenomenon. However, it'd be rather throwing themselves into risk and danger to help other people in need of the help. Sacrifice isn't needed to defy the phenomenon, but sacrifice would actually make it seem worse the problem since more deaths have occurred, if it has to occur, that is. Anyways, what really has to occur is the person taking risk and danger to help others, not sacrifice, don't get me wrong. You can see these outliers in public places, as in doing what normal people did not do in examples above. To show a new example, somebody had fallen into the subway railroad from the guardrail, and everyone, as expected, was taking videos on their phones, and watching the person in agony. However, someone appears, runs before the train gets too near, and picks the man up, and sprints into the guard rail saving the man and himself. This example might not occur as often as helping others pick up their properties, but it had occurred multiple times, in many countries around the world. They were risking their lives for a complete stranger, and almost every person, when interviewed whether they were scared that the train would hit them, they reply, 'I didn't really see the danger until the whole thing was over'. Therefore, after years of research, it has been proved that they were not especially more heroic people, although their actions were, it just they had different situation processing skills. Most people look at a scene, considering everything they can related to danger, however, those people do what is seems to be most important for the whole. They run to help, without noticing the danger and the risks at all, which surely is a mighty help for the person getting helped, but this, most people don't have, because the natural instincts of a human includes being alive effectively over others' safety.

The reason above is not the only reason people offer these kind of help. The people who have helped become the role models of the others. If one sees the heroic action in action, then they will willingly do the same if the saw it happen again. This has been shown multiple times around the world, and examples mentioned above, like the subway incident, the people of Japan, who saw a Korean man do the action, had saved many people from dying by doing the same. To add to the information, when interviewed, they had said "When a saw this man fall, I thought of the incident that I had seen on the newspaper and did the same thing he did."

Doing this, as I repeat, doesn't mean those people are any kinder or moral than you, they just perceive the world differently than most people. Although, they shan't be considered unheroic, as they did what most didn't do. It also means that you or anybody could be the hero, if you were willing to do so, and you don't have to be the hero we think of in our society, the kind and nice person. Therefore it is not a very good reasoning to say I can't be the person, I'm not good 'enough', or someone better will do it for me, since they've been better or will be.

A Short Introduction to Social Psychology

Obedience to Authority

This topic is a sort of social pressure that can be defied by actions like standing up for others and standing up for oneself to be correct, by not 'fitting in'. In fact, it is standing up for yourself, but not in Asch's way, or along with people that are believed to be in equal social state with you. This, as the title mentions, is quite harder than standing up for people in equal social state. It is because they are in higher social state than you, which means the people are not 'pushovers'. Although they are in authority, one must remember this: they do not have to be scary or intimidating to make others obey them, that would rather be something immoral and illegal. It's that part in the back of people's head that keeps causing this, they think that they themselves would benefit by obeying, since they are in authority, or that the people in authority might threaten them, even though most people in authority do not do that.

This can be observed through the all famous Milgram's Experiment, which is many times described as the most immoral social-psychological experiment. It is because of the concept of violence used in the people, although no literal assault was used. The experiment went like this: A brochure was spread saying people a participant (test marker) was needed for a memory experiment, and they were to be paid four dollars an hour, which was a lot at the time. In total forty people were chosen as the 'participants'. The people ranged from all couriers, including professors, white-collar workers, blue-collar workers, and businessmen. They all were to be tested on obedience.

When they got there, Milgram told the participants, that a test taker was behind the wall which they couldn't see through, and they were to ask the questions about the memory test through a mike. If the answer the participant gave was incorrect, they were to pull a lever on a machine, which in result would shock the participant. The shock was not a simple shock pen, but a big machine that had shocks ranging from 15 volts, labeled Simple Shock, to 450 volts of electricity, with big XXX markings on it, hinting the result being death (a typical shock pen consists around 50 volts). This was just hinting, and Milgram assured the participants no deaths or permanent tissue injury would occur on the people taking test, but is extremely painful.

However, since actual electric shock would result in assault and be illegal, Milgram decided that the electricity shouldn't actually applied on the test taker but should be acted out, and the participant wouldn't need to be worried and feel empathy for the test taker at all. This is the background of the terrifying experiment. When the experiment had started, the participants, although reluctant, started shocking the participant, every time they got the question wrong. The participant would react painfully every voltage, grunting and moaning until 75 voltages of electricity, then when at 150 volts, the participant asks if this experiment can be stopped due to the continuous sock, then at 180, he cries he can't stand the pain, and the yells, kicking the wall. Crying is added along with the higher voltages. As the reactions from the test taker (actor) was getting more painful and painful, there were objections from the participants. At the first objection, Milgram replied, "He's fine, go on," then, as the objections increased these were Milgram's words: "The experiment requires you to go on,", and then "It is absolutely essential that you go on" then finally, at the fourth reaction, "You have no choice, you must go on!" As the reader, what do you think is the number of people that applied 450 volts of electricity? When Milgram asked his fellow social psychologists, about forty of them, they concluded that less than one percent of the people would actually apply that much electricity. However, their guess was horribly incorrect. Sixty-eight percent of the appliers had pressed 450 volts unto the test takers, when no one had expected such obedience under such little pressure applied. The greater part is that everyone had conducted more than 350 volts, which is also quite fatal to a person if electrocuted continuously. Milgram had thought that since we were babies, it was embedded to us that to harm others in such a way, especially if it was against our will, was not to happen, and no one wouldn't do such thing. Although he was wrong, what this result proved was that obedience is part of our society and is natural human behavior, and has very strong power over us. There are many other factors to consider in this experiment, as an example, the fact that the experimenter was a scientist working at Yale University, and that the participants knew, that was a big deal, since everyone assumes no one is going to get harmed in an experiment made by a famous Ivy-League school, and think the results would be used for good. When the experimenter was replaced by a fellow participant, although the participant was an actor being a participant, the number stumbled down as low to 20 percent of the participants. That is considerably lower than the original, but still a very large number, considering the concept of the experiment. Then, the experimenter was replaced with calling from a far, even though it was more effective than a fellow participant experimenting, (25 percent) but most of the people who harmed had not taken the order properly. When they were asked to apply higher voltages upon the test taker, they had actually applied far lower voltages, since they didn't want to harm the test taker as much and minimize the harm made by themselves. This result proves Professor Milgram partially correct; since it was that we don't want to harm

A Short Introduction to Social Psychology

others and do have big empathy, but it was just that our obedience to others were stronger than our own feelings. Therefore, this experiment shouldn't confuse or make one think that humans are ruthless, non-sympathetic, emotionless animals. We are very social and respect each other in high value, but some effects in our brain differ from our usual selves, and they were evolved to make benefit to us.

This result made by the first experiment of Milgram many scientists question (although some don't consider psychologists scientists, in this book they will be considered scientists since psychology is also a big field of study along with biology, chemistry, physics, etc..) why does obedience occur, although that wasn't the main point of the experiment, and we didn't get to know. What we do know is that these people weren't disabled, sadistic, or had noticed that the test was an experiment, and they weren't just plainly mean, but was because

of obedience that caused this. In fact, when the participants were tested in normal personality tests, the people who rejected and the people who continued on had very similar results. Also, none of them had stayed calm during the experiment, some objected to continue, man people showed signs of nervousness and worriedness by sweating, stuttering, and trembling. This result and observations weren't just in Connecticut America (where the experiment was conducted), but when the experiment was repeated around the world (Australia, Jordan, Spain, UK, Germany, Japan, and the Netherlands, etc…) to see if the result was accurate, and the results were very similar. There was very little difference in result between genders when tested on women, since Milgram had selectively experimented on men.
Another fact they've figured is what obedience causes. Obedience causes order, which usually many of our instincts causes something positive, but this isn't

necessarily positive. However, this causes us to work together in harsh environments that would have been good in the very olden days, but obedience and order has also caused many destructive and inhumane affects like the German Nazis and their death camps, which is the most extreme case of obedience to authority. This also proves that anyone could be part of something very devastating or inhumane if psychological effects are in action. It's proven because the German people were not borne evil, they weren't very different from the people of Poland or Austria, which they took over, it's the atmosphere and cultural education they had gotten. This can be seen in many different events, one mentioned is the people in Abu Ghraib, the people who had caused the problem, when asked, replied they were obeying orders from the superior authorities, whom had called them 'bad apples'. The people were very innocent, although they were in the army, meaning there is difference in psychological effects compared to an average citizen. Many events like this happened in the army, another example of this is in Vietnam, during its war, when the American soldiers brutally murdered the women and the children of Vietnam, they were also following orders. Even though they were soldiers and were trained to kill, they were less reluctant to killing and seeing other people get harmed then average citizens, it does not change the meaning obedience is very powerful to human society and its people.

Other Uses and Experiments about Obedience to Authority

Although Milgram's experiment might be very interesting to look at, there are many other experiments about this topic, since it does not quite fit along with what we think about ourselves, and therefore, in this chapter, other intriguing ideas about Obedience will be viewed.

Firstly, it should be known that scientists aren't the only people who cause obedience to the common people. There are many in authority in our current society, including police officers, doctors, government leaders, and the people of the military. There would be many more if listed, since some people obey to others whom which they need not obey to.

Doctors, are not threatening figures unlike many other people in authority, but we obey them since they have much more knowledge than we do, and the knowledge is quite important to our lives since it includes fatal bodily information. Therefore, we tend to obey their orders because we do not know what they are doing, and what we are being asked to do. As an example, a group of scientists decided to experiment how much people would listen to the doctor ordering nonsense to the people on checkup. The commands were like please take off your shoes and glasses, and please hold the heaviest object near you for 20 seconds. These are commands I made up, but the actual commands were very similar to this, if not less comprehendible. The results were quite amazing; no one had even questioned why they were doing all the nonsense, they were just expecting that it would be something important and complying to the nonsense. Therefore this shows that knowledge is power, and everyone will follow you if you have important knowledge. If knowledge gives one power, then it could and will be used as bad by somebody, which means one might and someone will, commit crimes using this power, and is seen in many cases where doctors harass their patients, or assault other patients. This may be done because many people assume that people in authority will use information for good and be good (except maybe the government), although that is many times incorrect, since they are maybe more educated but bear the same feelings and emotions as everyone does. France even has a word for it, noblesse oblige, which means at the time, people in high authority, like the aristocrats, should act noble and moral to the common people, which obviously wasn't the case. The English Language plainly admits it without having to have a word, by saying, 'you're older, act like your age', 'be a man, not some sissy', 'act like you are a (job), not some (job)', this means that the subjects are in authority, which when the sentences were made they were, and since grammar was made after language, we can tell that everyone expected 'high people act noble', since it's included in the language.

This has caused much more trouble, because one does not need to be in high authority to seem like one is in high authority, there have been many imitations of this sort. The reason for imitation would be to cause offence of any sort, and in many ways. In the United States, instead of robbing or hijacking a store, the criminals decided that it would be better to imitate as a cop. Since more can be expected and more details can be seen by the when physically being there, even though it is that it is less effective, the criminals called the restaurant and told there were cops, and they were getting there for a checkup of some sort and the owner were to take all the money out. Although this may sound like nonsense, when a scary cop says to do something, many obey, and this can be proven through the drink-and-driving checkup. People cannot even walk in a straight line because they're too scared,

A Short Introduction to Social Psychology

which means they are in quite very high authority, and not many drive right through the cops, but they actually take the fine even though they could've (although very, very illegal) drove past if they wanted too. Getting back on topic, the people in the store followed as the criminals ordered, since they believed that it was a real checkup since the emotions make the frontal cortex choose less and the amygdala, where the natural instincts are placed, choose more. After taking the money out, many orders were placed to harass and strip other workers and steal from them, which they obeyed, resulting in more harm. After they ordered, the criminals never resulted in getting to the restaurant, but rather running away. It was harder for the cops since they had used the public phone. Other than this, there were many cases of harassment done through the telephone, imitating to be in person of authority, which resulted in most of the criminals getting caught, but it still remains one of the most effective ways of theft.

If one has a thought that they should look out for imitators acting to be in authority, then one is wrong. That is because no one is to be not looked carefully if they're in authority, because we follow their instructions without thinking very much. This is the power of the human race, teamwork without thinking very much, especially on children. However, if we use this in a negative way like Nazi Germany, bad results will happen. Therefore, before following instructions, one must look for why this task was given, and whether or not the task given is a correct task to follow. What this means is that one must not expect the people in authority to be trustworthy or honest, since they, with enough power and greed, will turn in to something nobody had seen before. Concluding the chapter, I'm trying to note that one should not expect anything from anyone, or trust anyone's commands.

A Short Introduction to Social Psychology

Deception of Mind

We see what we want to see, we hear what we want to hear, and we believe what we want to believe. Every day, our mind tricks us by making us believe the false, and deny the truth. No one looks at the world equally, because it is full of opinions they made, or locked in the boundaries of their communities. During the cold war, not many Americans would've thought the Russians were friendly, or Russians to think that Americans were very friendly, even though there isn't evidence one of which is friendlier, and in our little capitalist world, many people think Russia is the 'bad guy', from the standards we made for our society. With all these deceptions we think of our world the way we want it to be, which doesn't necessarily mean good, but the way we want to think about it. No one does not have opinions, since we all have emotion, we are not artificial intelligence, and we are natural intelligence. Therefore the judges of our world, UN administrators who make important decisions for the world, will have opinions that either hold us back, push us forward, or trick us into thinking one of them (usually the latter). This is linked to obedience to authority. Since we follow authority easily, and if someone said an opinion they believed in, we should believe that it is true more easily, and get persuaded more easily, because believing in their opinion is also following their orders.

This can be seen through the Propaganda's of many places, but this may be seen very visibly in Nazi Germany. Nazi Germany is repeated many times in this book because social-psychological manipulation is seen very extensively through this, especially if it is about authority. Adolf Hitler himself, as a propaganda strategist, had mentioned that propagandas are a truly terrible weapons at a hands of the expert, and this

A Short Introduction to Social Psychology

was used to deceive people in to thinking about the utopian European world that would be fantastic, and threatening pictures of the enemy that looks like it would be a blockage to the utopian world. They also confused them and tricked them about war and how necessary and not harmful it was too the world, in fact, that war would push them in to a better place. They even handed knives and pins to the bows of their Youth Groups, which made the children don't feel very horrified about goriness. It is related to parents telling that there is too much goriness in videogames these days, how long exposures could make children feel dull and decrease seriousness of war and killing (this has been proven correct to a degree). These may feel very simplistic, but all the steps the political party took was very sophisticated, and was enough to lead them in to a party in power.

Sometimes, we get deceived by our brains simply because we don't sense it. Even though it is said that we may multitask, we cannot concentrate everything on what we receive from our multiple senses. If we concentrate on doing our test, we would not notice if the teacher was changed. If we were listening to motorcycles, we would not hear bird calls. Many people probably can relate to this one; we would not hear our moms call for dinner, if we were so deeply interested in our great books. This, many call mistakes or misunderstanding because the word deceiving may be misleading to some people. Everyone is missing out on something because of this, and this happens constantly in each person, no matter what they are missing out on, big or small, even Bill Gates or Warren Buffett. This is because we forget many of our experiences and input from our world, and limited amount of information do our senses send to our brain, which then is remembered for a limited amount of time.

A Short Introduction to Social Psychology

Once, a Korean broadcasting station did an experiment during a documentary where they tried if citizens in Seoul recognized if people were switched during an event. For example, we see a person asking the route to a place holding a map. Then all of a sudden, people holding a large object passes between them, and the person asking the question is switched with another person with equivalent attire. This was to test how many noticed that the person had changed. The mainstream guess would be that everyone would notice, if a whole new body had appeared. This again, like in many famous experiments is a far off guess. At first the person asking the person, a young man in the twenties, is switched with another man in the twenties. They had similar hair, not many had noticed with all minding their businesses. Then, they switched the new person changed to an older man in the fifties. Think more will notice? Actually, there wasn't a very big difference between the first trial. Finally, at the final trial, they switched gender, (although they had recruited a short haired woman) and even with people with different gender, high tone and low tone, only 80 percent of the people asked routes for had admitted they had noticed that a new person had appeared in the middle of it, when being interviewed after.

One may think the meeting of the people were too short for other people to notice, and so the broad casting station had done a variation of an experiment; now, the setting was in the doctor's office where people came for a checkup. At there, the doctor asked real checkup questions this time, not random questions, but in the middle of the experiment, he dropped his pen, acting naturally, as if he was playing with it. Then, when he crawls under the desk to reach the pen, another doctor appears as if he dropped the pen, and this again sees who notices the different people.

A Short Introduction to Social Psychology

When we remember things, we forget things at the same time; this is proven through neuroscience, and therefore this makes it easier to confuse other people. As an example, if I were to falsely make a chart of every time my friends and I had a meal together and told them that at June 7th, 2014, they had spaghetti, it is very hard to deny the fact, since people forget what they ate long time ago, let alone yesterday. Or, if I were to say we played tennis together a month ago with a very specific date, it is hard to deny it, since they had forgotten. This may seem like nothing, and it will to most people, since it is one of the least things manipulation about this topic can do. Millenniums ago this little deceiving of memory could have changed world history, by making the community think a ruler hundred years ago had committed a crime that we all remember somewhat of. A few may have argued, but then they were held in court for disagreeing with the ruler. This would be the cooperation between pre-modern age logic and deceiving of the mind. One could also use a way to free themselves from something against their want, and as an example if one wanted to end work early, they could argue that we had missed a day off, which in most cases they would have to work anyways, it doesn't really matter at work, but what is possible is confusing your co-workers into make your co-workers expect something very absurd for lunch, that it was planned all along and they just don't remember the announcement made. These probably still don't sound very serious, but to give a serious example, Nero, an emperor of Rome, many people think he played his lovely fiddle while Rome was burning in flames. This is proved a fraud, and the next emperors had reasons to do so. Nero, through geographical founding, was the emperor who researched (hired people) and rebuilt the burnt Rome with proper concrete so the buildings were sturdier

A Short Introduction to Social Psychology

against fire, but then why would anyone accuse him with such horrible vandalism? The best guess would be the succeeding emperors, to get the positive public opinion away from Nero and to themselves, which would mean there would be less civil wars, rebels, less argument, and easily getting people's agreement. In current days, it would mean more citizens following laws, easily passing bills and possibly getting votes to be president again. With such power of changing big events in history, we can use other's brains to benefit us; for we do not have photogenic memory.

This effect also worked in recent times, during the post-globalization period, at Los Angeles Korea town, America. The event that occurred is quite famous, and involved much damage. This started with a shooting. A Korean convenience store owner (Female, Name: Soon Ja Du) had been going through much thefts, and it was mostly American-Africans, and therefore, when a teenage girl Latasha Harlins had put a soft drink in her bag without paying, which she noticed, then she owner decided to take her backpack. This resulted in a fight quite big, they were swearing at each other, and were quite noticeable to witnesses, and the teenager punched the owner four times, one of her blows had made the owner's eye swell, and with the same blow she fell. After retrieving the bag, the teenager put the stolen drink on the counter and walked to leave peacefully, the store owner had pulled out a gun and fired. The bullet hit the girl's head, and she had died at the place. Therefore she was sent to the local court, and the prosecutors had put her in 5 years of prison and a bail of $250 000 USD, and accused her of murder. Even this might seem too little of a punishment for some because to kill a person because they had punched you seems very unfair and unreasonable, but this incident had counted as legitimate self-defense by the local judges. In their

A Short Introduction to Social Psychology

reasoning documents it was recorded "Judge Karlin reasoned that Soon Ja Du and her family had been terrorized by crime that her response to Latasha Harlins, shooting her in the back of her head, was reasonable." In people words, it means Ms. Du could have been confused that she was a scary person of threat, and it was quite reasonable to kill her. Then the punishment she gotten was a fine of $500, five years of probation, and four hundred hours of community service. This might be correct for Ms. Du because of so much thefts, but to be on Latasha Harlin's side, then it is a totally different story. She was a very innocent girl attending a normal high school, and she was one of the top students of the school. Then, to be shot because the shop owner was confused whether she was a thief or not, and die, that's very unfair. Also, this incident happened right after a video was released, about a police beating Rodney King, and showed unfairness between ethics. Therefore, in Los Angeles there was a very big riot with more than 2000 injuries, and armed police being put, and 65 percent of the damaged properties were of Korean owners. It took very long to recover from this, and after decades, still video tapes showing beatings because of ethics are being released, which means the big problem still hasn't been fixed. However, about Soon Ja Du, her store had never reopened, and the case was over like that. This is the power of deceiving the mind, confusing them, even without anyone purposely trying to, and many times results in riots and deaths like this.

The deceiving power is great against people with low self-esteem, since they don't trust themselves any more than they trust others, or people with low ego, since they will more willingly follow orders and believe in them. As so, like many psychological studies, manipulation rates of others vary among communities and individuals. For example, people in Eastern Asia, where cultures think (or at least thought, since it is there in the history before our westerners) individualism is odd, unnecessary or overwhelming, obedience rates are much higher, since 'peace' with the group has been untouched. There is such a big difference, there are studies about which, and it has shown they do think differently. In fact, during the Milgram Experiment, when conducted at Japan, their obedience rate (the people who conducted more than 450 volts electricity to the victims) was more than 85%. This means there is about a 20 percent difference between the two cultures, one in five person being obedient in Japan, which means the population of North Korea is more obedient, giving the country more order. There are also a slight difference in obedience between genders, of which women being somewhat more obedient, but the difference is very low to be noticeable during actual casual life. When there are differences like this, it makes group manipulation harder, and so one shan't think it is easy, as I repeat, or try it in many cases, since many experiment is morally incorrect. However, if one's trying to take their friend's cookies, try everything given in this book; for everyone loves cookies.

A Short Introduction to Social Psychology

Chris Park

The Deceiving in Our Beliefs

One might be deceived by outer inputs given to them, but in many cases, people get deceived every day because they do not realize many facts and can only think about incidents in one perspective, themselves. Therefore, they get lost so much in their thought and problems, they don't realize other people are doing the same, getting lost in their thought and problems. This means people actually think that others care about them, and I don't mean their family doesn't care about them, but I mean strangers passing by at the mall or a restaurant do not care. It is because if they actually did care about every single person that pass by them, then their brain would reach maximum capacity. Those people do not care about other strangers, as they have special people to care about like their family. However, someone might argue there was one single person was staring at them at the mall, but that doesn't change much, because despite the fact they might think about you for a while, no one will question you or remember it for a long time. We are forgetters. This forgetfulness, can also be taken to the extreme measures by our interesting experiments.

One team had tested on how many people cared about others' fashions. They had consented a group of people to watch a basketball game with a slight twist; they had to wear a one-piece spandex suit. To get a visual perspective, it looked like the Green Men on the Vancouver Hockey Team, Canucks, which was once famous, or the professional bicyclists which can be seen at major competitions like Tour de France. The full spandex suit, would make anyone feel embarrassed in a group of people they do not know, or business partners might be there, and the people were sent alone to increase the emotions of the participants. At first, most people, after entering the stadium, were too embarrassed to move anywhere than a little seat at the corner. Then, to maximize the emotions, the participants were ordered to move around the stadium, maybe walking in front of rows that were full of people, or buy some popcorn where they sell food. These were very mentally heavy tasks for average adults to do, and of course many were very embarrassed, but the results they got from other people who were viewing the basketball game were absolutely unexpected. After the game, the experimenters asked the people who watched the game if they saw a person wearing a spandex suit walking around, and most of the people had replied they hadn't noticed much, and so they asked the specific people who were caught on tape looking at the people in the spandex suits for some time. Again, some said they don't really remember it, and most didn't really seem to care about it, expecting the participants to have a fair reason for doing so.

This very basic experiment can show much information about how we think of ourselves in our society and our beliefs about them. Firstly, we can see that our belief about society can change our feelings, as people who participated said they felt like everyone was eyeing them, and were all talking about them. The social embarrassment had also blocked their ability to think clearly about anything else than the clothing they were wearing, which meant they didn't had the ability to analyze everything they saw, and weren't able to judge analytically whether others were actually caring or not, which leads to the second information received from this experiment.

Secondly, we can see that most, if not everyone, believes that other people care about them a lot, and this is probably due to the fact, the basic knowledge we have, which is that everything is about me, me, and me. The world

A Short Introduction to Social Psychology

revolves around me, and I am the center of the universe. This is a humorous way of putting that we can't literally be in someone else's shoes, without actually being them, because we can't read minds or be in the minds. On the internet, there is a quote, saying that everyone has three faces, one of which you show to the world, one shown to the family, and the final one if only kept to yourself, and is the truest self. This practically says that you can't be in someone else's shoes, they keep it locked away only for themselves. Therefore we have to rely on our beliefs about the thoughts of other people about us, and this is very hard, since no one really knows, and no one is willing to share their own truest thoughts. Then, it is safe to assume some, if not most, of our beliefs about others are wrong.

This is quite surprising because we trust others and our family to be honest, in many of the cases they think they are, but are so used to hiding their truthful selves, without even noticing they can be hidden. However, we hide our own selves to everyone, and so it's not just others that's untrustworthy, it's everyone. The last word was everyone, since it includes every one and each person, including themselves. Our mind tricks our beliefs about us, not just others. As an example, in most of human skills, we think we are above average than everyone else, which is incorrect, since almost everyone is average, and tend to rate ourselves lower than reality to specific people, like friends, since we know them close enough to know they're better or we are better by a hair. This effect, which many seem negative to some people, gives us the ability to improve and get better in a competition.

The other things we tend to believe easily is the information about us given by others, or what we make up. The information given by others, if positive, then one is very likely to believe the information, for example, if a psychology doctor had talked to one that they were potentially good at math, and were congenitally kind to others, then one is most likely to believe it, since we all think we are nice to others, have good manners, and think we are better than others at many subjects. On the other hand, if the psychologist said one is very shy, is very lower than average at studying languages, and doesn't have any potential in music, then one wouldn't believe that, since they do not want to, and that is because the information given was negative.

To make the negative information sound realistic, showing proof will support the result, even if no logical reasoning is given. The definition of proof in this context is that one may get some basic information about the people before giving out fake information, like asking the favorite color or a fingerprint of theirs. To them, this might seem like absurd info to get, but as explained on the obedience to authority chapter, we tend to believe things more easily if we have no idea of how it works. Therefore, if any information is gotten beforehand telling the participant fake information, the likelihood of modifying their belief is increased. Another way to increase this factor is to take time, giving the participant the thought 'this person is actually thinking about my personality, and is not writing random facts that come out of their mind'. This is linked to thinking that other people care about everyone, since that is what causes this person to think this matter that other people actually took the time to think about their personality. The final reason gets the matter in to pure lying and tricking, which is giving fake reasons with information to support the information. This is harder to accomplish because it requires time to put in to trick others, think of reasons why this nonsense makes sense. This is how fortune telling works, giving the people fake information that seemingly appears to be true because they are either positive, or very general and applies to almost everyone or even everything. This is an interesting concept because as mentioned, we believe what we want to believe, and what we want to take in. Then, why would we believe someone else's opinion, which is not ours, and some things we don't want to be true?

Again, everything matters in the knowledge about the topic. If one knows lot about their personality and oneself, then one would not get persuaded by fortune tellers or personality tests. However, this is quite impossible, because we cannot measure it by numbers, and it changes as time passes. Therefore, if one knew their personality well in their mid-twenties, then it might be completely opposite in their mid-forties, and no one can be hundred percent sure about their personality. To know their personality well is valued as a great advantage in our society; hence relying on other people/things to figure out for them is seemingly quite easier and efficient. Depending on how efficient someone believes this is, or in other words, how much their unsure about themselves, changes how much and easily a person can be persuaded. Including another factor, if people have an opinion about themselves, it makes persuading them the most hard, since psychologically, not many are

A Short Introduction to Social Psychology

willing to easily get rid of their opinion, since that would mean they were wrong, and no one likes to be wrong. The opinion does not have to be correct to stick with someone, what matters is whether that opinion is strong or not, since that is another variable to consider. Then, to get everyone believing, one of the psychological tricks the personality testing industry is using is telling general ideas that sound specific. This means telling ideas everyone have like you are nice, but adding a few adjectives or adjective phrases and clauses to sound specific. An example of this would be: "You were nice to everyone *since you were a child*" The italics part, describes the person more specifically by giving the 'when' part of the sentence. There are many ways like this to tricking people from the personality testing industry.

Then, many started to wonder why people are tricked in to seemingly easy-to-find tricks or confusions as the basketball game experiment, like how we get confused if people are looking at us or not. The results of this came from the neuroscientists. Firstly, it is hard to find, since we get about ten million different information from our five senses, and only forty of them are saved in to our brain. This would mean our brain involuntarily edits the information we remember, meaning everything is hard to find, because

we don't get to choose what is saved. Interestingly, our brain makes finding those schemes even harder, by missing a sensor that would be great to have. Our brain does not have a sensor to detect exceptions. That's why we can see visual illusions like magic eye, and can't find what is true and what's not, or what's false information like how people were embarrassed for no reason in the basketball game and what's actual damage to social reputation and should be embarrassed about. Without all these disadvantages in the brain, we would be superior animals we are now, making us harder to get persuaded and give us more advantage, but these mistakes in our genes are what gives humans humaneness.

A Short Introduction to Social Psychology

Psychological Selfishness

We are all selfish creatures. As seen in experiments above, we only like to believe what we want to, and see what we want to. Taking in other people's opinions that is opposite of mine is hard and sharing our opinions so others believe is hard since we know it's hard for them to believe. The root of this comes from selfishness, where we like to think from our prospective. Selfishness, is not the definition of people who don't share or take other people's property. That has another set of words, like mean, rude, and manner less. Selfishness is quite different, it's not caring about other's feelings or perspective. As mentioned earlier in this book, we cannot be in someone else's shoes, that's quite impossible, and that's what caused people to get deceived, untrue information about other's perspective giving our brain confusion.

A Short Introduction to Social Psychology

There is another kind of selfishness, which is indirect, so to some it might not seem like selfishness right away, and that is the fact that we think we are special. We think probability is in our favor. For example, we think we will be the ones to win the lottery, win all our bets in the casino (gambling), and we even think most of the things we wish to happen will happen. This also happens the other way around, where people think they are especially unlucky, and blame that for the negative happenings in their life. For example, where the people fault their positions in life, like a cashier, and they became one because they were unlucky on their finals test. This is different from superstition, since superstition may be applied to everyone, whereas this selfishness is modified differently be each person.

The inequality we think that exists between other people and our society ranges quite a lot, because some people realize that they are not special enough to get special treatment from the world before thinking they are lucky or unlucky. However, most of the people like to blame everything in their lives, (mostly bad events) to the natural occurrences, or occurrences made by other people. This blaming starts from that it is easier to blame everything, and the puzzle piece seems to fit them if the selfishness part is thrown in.

This selfishness, might seem very useless, and everyone needs to improve on it, but this could be considered as a key. We all have the ability to think that we are special beings, and this key can open many doors. The result of opening this door may catastrophic, or it could make the best event of your life. The reason is that, the selfishness, the way we deceive ourselves that we are important, drives the dopamine from our brain, it causes happiness. This happiness may turn in to hope, that you can do something that seems to be impossible.

A Short Introduction to Social Psychology

This small piece of hope from small pieces of people was the engine that drove us with our new technology and innovation, and although deceiving ourselves might sound unintelligent, it is still good for our human society to have a little bit of that, to improve an take new limits.

Chris Park

Reciprocity

Firstly, I'd like to go over what reciprocity, [resəˈpräsədē] means, since some readers couldn't have known or is misunderstanding this word. This word, is where the phrase give and take comes from, and also where 'revenge is sweet' comes from. This phenomenon is the bond that keeps us together in our interpersonal relationships. When we give others something, we are losing that something, and if we are losing something, humans need a reason for it. As an example, this is where debt is specified, because when the bank loses money, it gets it back. However, many people gives gifts to each other for no reason, as it seems. This, we still earn something by doing this, and it may be something better than physical reward. The reward is the stronger interpersonal relationship with them, also known as getting closer to them. Working together to achieve a goal, or helping each other on hard times, is why interpersonal relationship may be important to one.

To touch a bit of evolutionary psychology, we humans needed reciprocity since the ancient times. If we were to rely solely on our emotions, or group activity, then one would keep giving to the poor until nothing was left for oneself. On the other hand, if one was to rely solely on logic, or competition, then one would die due to natural causes while others would survive by helping each other out. Therefore the people without this ability would've had a less chance of surviving, and the number of people without it would've decreased rampantly.

The cooperative element of ourselves, is the reason why we make friends so effectively, but it can also bring us to our knees. Reciprocity behaves like many other piece of the universe we've discovered, and has two sides. We give others positive gifts; for they have done so, and we try to equal the value of the gifts exchanged. However, this is like an integer; we give others negative things; for they have done so, and we try to equal the value of the things exchanged. It is the fundamental basis of retaliation, or revenge. To apply anger at one, means the other has to lose something, and reciprocity is when the other decides to get it back by applying their anger, which does not always work, as seen on dramatic storylines.

Overall, reciprocity helped us evolve and get through our hard times, although arguable. It helped us cooperate in the hard times, or the so called dark ages, and prosper ourselves (and our genes) effectively. When we were to lose something, it helped us get it back, if not, it taught not to do negative things to each other by both of them losing something.

A Short Introduction to Social Psychology

Chris Park

Deceiving in the Marketing Industry

We see many applications of the phenomenon's learned in social psychology being used as marketing strategies for many large, blue chip companies. It is very easy to find connections between these two topics, and because most of us don't notice it, the more likely, and easy for companies to do.

Firstly, let's use the first topic this book has gone over, conformity. Some people call it the 'me too' effect, because many people are likely to buy it after many others have tried. This was mentioned before, as the power of three {(no, not $3^\wedge x$), but this($x>3$), the power as in strength}, and how few people can cause a huge traffic jam, just by looking at something (full of curiosity) in the middle of a crosswalk. In the marketing industry, this is caused because the people, at first, have a doubt about a product, and will not buy it, because they have to pay, which means they're losing something, and

A Short Introduction to Social Psychology

reciprocity is not there. Elsewise, one might've not known, or didn't have interest in the product, but bought it by the sole fact of others having it, where others means anyone ranging from celebrities to friends. That, is called a trend.

These, are literally everywhere, and are easy to find. Marketers do it by posting blogs, vlogs, or sharing it on SNS. It can pop up as reviews (tons of it for dieting pills or fitness clubs), or simply people sharing it. This is how many benefit from retweets. However, the main place to look for, are sponsors. Everything a celebrity does and wears is probably related to sponsorship, and the people who conform are immeasurable. This is why in many countries celebrities shoot TV ads, it has a better chance of people conforming if celebrities 'use the product'.

Secondly, obedience to authority is also a very tactful. Most of the ethics in marketing is through obedience to authority, where it is said 'FDA proved', '000 certified', or scientists might say why this product must be used. To give a comparison, just saying 'proven to be the best drink', versus the same thing plus what university/organization it was researched and who with what major has studied, more people will buy the latter. People like this proof, it gives a sensation that they know well about the product, and the product is trustworthy.

One other use of this would be explaining the ethics of the authority. Authority, in marketing, comes as many different couriers, but mostly, the maker of the product will do. This means for books, it would be authors, for big companies, it would be the C.E.O. (s). By describing the ethics of that person, the effect it gives to customers is this: 'If that amazing person has made it, it'd be reasonable enough to buy', or 'If such a person made a product, it must be good'. Then, buying is made in no time, with the trust they have earned.

With all the information, it is possible to conclude that while people are obeying to authority, buying their products and doing what they want you to do, they think they are in control, that they are in authority.

A Short Introduction to Social Psychology

This, as written before, by giving out the ethics of the authority, and making people trust the authority, is the way authority gets more power. When repeating this method, the authority may become higher authority. Lastly, a chapter about reciprocity was dealt with, but it is still a quite often used method in marketing. This give and take may seem like it doesn't exist, that the customers pay for the product and that's it. However, there are many examples of this, like that buy one get one free deals, the chance to win this buy buying our product, that loyalty program like free burger for 12 stamps, is all a sort of reciprocity. The examples are probably self-explanatory, but to go over them, the buy one get one free means we are giving your money back, (which they actually might be selling a product for twice the amount), or in a different representation, we are giving you a free t-shirt. Next, the lottery method is probably most effective way of reciprocity, if one wins, since they got the 'take' part first, and most will be generous enough to fill the equation with the 'give part'. Finally, the most common way of reciprocity, is the loyalty program 'available at any store that is big enough to have one', which uses probably the most direct method, where it's when you give this, this, and that to me, I'll give you this lovely gift! (Usually it doesn't result in being all that lovely but in fact useless, or unnoticeable, like 2% of that jacket, or 10 dollars of that TV. This is great, since it makes the customer keep buying, reaching for that gift. It is legit enough to believe that this method actually controls human instincts quite effectively. Using the fact that the human likes to get back what the lost (paid) companies act like they are giving something back, and makes the person buy things repetitively, for a gift that is almost nothing. It is much effective than someone coming once for a quick sale.

A Short Introduction to Social Psychology

Chris Park

A Short Introduction to Social Psychology